The Art Of Living A Perfect Way Of Life

A Short Guide To Living A New Way Of Life

Jayani Mattu

ISBN 978-93-5610-886-8
© Jayani Mattu 2022
Published in India 2022 by Pencil

A brand of
One Point Six Technologies Pvt. Ltd.
123, Building J2, Shram Seva Premises,
Wadala Truck Terminal, Wadala (E)
Mumbai 400037, Maharashtra, INDIA
E connect@thepencilapp.com
W www.thepencilapp.com

All rights reserved worldwide

No part of this publication may be reproduced, stored in or introduced into a retrieval system, or transmitted, in any form, or by any means (electronic, mechanical, photocopying, recording or otherwise), without the prior written permission of the Publisher. Any person who commits an unauthorized act in relation to this publication can be liable to criminal prosecution and civil claims for damages.

DISCLAIMER: *The opinions expressed in this book are those of the authors and do not purport to reflect the views of the Publisher.*

Author biography

Warm Greetings dear readers!

I am pleased to share my second book with all of you. I am happy to see myself growing as a writer with each of my publications. I am a young girl in school and aspire to explore possibilities in the field of writing. I am a Libra born on September 29. I know five languages and I am an avid follower of soccer. I write poems and newspaper articles. I am interested in science and fond of music. I play a few musical instruments. my previous book was ' the journey to Mallorca, this time I thought of writing a book that is so close to life and explains the ups and downs in life. lastly, I would like to thank you all for spending your precious time reading my book. I would love to hear feedback you can write it on my Gmail-jayanimattu2009@gmail.com

Thank You!

CONTENTS

Preface

After I finished writing my first book; I was thinking about the idea for my next book. Modern times have pushed people into a zone of anxiety and a habit of over-thinking which further leads to a stressed life among the youngsters. I decided to write a book to help others come out of their anxiety zones and know that they are special. I just took out my computer and started writing a book on it. It nearly took 2 weeks to complete. I wanted others to know that life has many normal things and most of them make us feel bad. I want others to believe in them. to know what they are meant to be. to be the one they always wanted despite their past or disabilities. I always wanted to help people and that's what makes me happy. I just now hope that this book is an inspiring one and it gives you an idea to progress in life without not letting your problems stop you. Thank You

Acknowledgements

As I have said earlier. I always believe that in the making of a young mind many people put effort to make one's dream come true. Just like that, first of all, my mother was always there to support me. though she has a lot of work to do she still takes time to help me fulfill my dreams. she gave me the idea to write a book when my parents got to know about my writing talent. my mother is like my heart if she's not here then I would not have been alive. she helps me and her unfailing support and unconditional love was the key I am here right now. then, my father was always there at my back. he gave me the courage and motivated me. He also helped me to lift higher in life. He always gives me everything that I want without even thinking for a second! everything I want I get it without asking. My school and teachers taught me many life lessons so that I become a responsible citizen. My aunts and my grandparents always cared for me and motivated me. thank you everyone for being there for me.
THANK YOU

Introduction

Hello dear readers! So here I present my 2nd book. This is an inspirational book in which I share with you how can we make our lives better and live a perfect way of life. So first of all I present you a summary to let you know about the chapters that are present in the book

CHAPTER 1

This chapter is an overview of what is life in the present. Here I will tell you that life comes one time so live it with full happiness and freedom.

CHAPTER 2

In this chapter, I tell you how good habits are important for you to live happily and also how it helps in shaping your life. Habits are very important in life as it represents us as a responsible citizen in society.

CHAPTER 3

In this chapter, I tell that relationship. also, play an important role in our lives as we grow we go through many relationships both good and bad. So, I tell you how we can live a good relationship and stay happy with our close ones.

CHAPTER 4

In this chapter, I take you through all the important things for your mental health and how to take care of it.

CHAPTER 5

In this chapter, I tell you how we can understand our true potential. That is who we are and how to decide our goals. I explain each step to understand your potential and how to succeed in life.

CHAPTER 6

In this chapter, I explain how can we live our dreams with full freedom and liberty. And achieve our goals by not staying under pressure but by our hearts.

CHAPTER 7

Here I explain how we can Take care of ourselves. Both mentally and physically. And stay healthy, happy, and cheerful always.

CHAPTER 8

Letting go of any pain isn't easy. So here I show you how we can let go of any pain and sorrow that comes into your life.

LIFE

Life, what is it? A gift? Well, many people say that it's true. Life is a gift. But not for the ones who waste their life and didn't take time to start their dreams over again. Some people think that I just don't want to live! Honestly most. Even some are so depressed they commit suicide?! But have you ever thought that because of any bad thing that happened to you; you will give your life instead?!

Just take a few minutes to think about what you are. What are you meant to be? What is the reason that God has given you this chance to live, life? Life's not a game. But somewhat like it. There are levels in a game, just like the steps you take. 'game over' means that you failed in completing the level. But, does this 'game over' means that you can't try again? In a game, you can try again if you lose the level, and then if you try, you will complete it! And make it to the next level! Just like is life. Ups and downs come sometimes things are just like a 'game over' but you can try again. Can't you?

This example is just to tell you. That life comes one time. There's one chance to live it. but please, because of these sorrows and pain that come, don't spoil it! try again, trying again is the key to being successful! The more you will try, the more opportunities will come! The more you will cry, the more you waste your life and the road to success. Life is like a storybook. The thing common, both are like a story only but the thing uncommon is that life is real and you can live it but storybooks aren't real. Those are Fiction created by people.

People are different, everyone. Some are smart, some are average looking, some are mentally strong and some are not. Just like 'beauty is in the eye of the beholder everyone has a different way of seeing things. And that's the thing which makes everyone special. If there is only one kind of animal, then who will be attracted to and love them? who wants to be bored by seeing only one?

A peacock is graceful dancing in the rain but without opening its feathers how will we see its inner beauty? The true beauty in a peacock is hidden in its feathers. So, if it keeps his feathers close and dances then would not be much graceful. Just like that! you are not graceful hiding your true colors beneath. Open your wings, fly high, and show your inner beauty to the world! And show that you are better than them. always try to be high!

To live a perfect way of life -never give up! Never compare yourself to others, everyone has different talents. Live your life with liberty and finally always try and never lose hope.

HABITS

You all might be thinking that what do habits do? How are they helpful in living a perfect way of life? Well, they play an important role as well! Firstly, good habits also are a path to success. If a person is well- mannered there are more chances of him getting successful and living happily. First, answer this question you had a job that a new trainee has joined your office and you have to guide him and tell him about your work. It was lunchtime and everybody went for it.

You took the trainee with you. You put on your apron and ate nicely. But, your trainee……. Lack of manners! Eating badly, dropping food on his clothes, and chewing loudly! Would you like to eat or stay with him? probably most of you will say no! well that's how manners are especially important for your success and contribution to society.

Everyone wants to stay with a well-mannered person and your manners will make you more popular and respected in society. Manners also show how are your personality and your knowledge too! There's never too late to start learning.

Now are good habits. Some of them include:

- Waking and sleeping early

- Keeping cleanliness

- Eating healthy food

- Exercising

- Learning new things

- Respecting others

And much more...........
Bad habits are the habits that not only make your personality development less but also affect your health. some bad habits include

- smoking

- usage of alcohol

- very much screen time

- no overall cleanliness

- staying up late at night etc.

you can try and remove these bad habits. Well, it's not possible that a person may have all the good habits. If a person may have many, he will have bad habits too. but still, you have to try to avoid these bad habits in public as well as practice these at home.
bad habits affect your health by:

- usage of alcohol affects your brain as it makes it difficult for your brain to create long-term memories. you also feel numbness and tingling etc.

- smoking damages your entire cardiovascular system. it high the blood pressure etc

- screen time affects your eyes.

- not being clean can make you sick as germs can enter your body.

- staying up late at night decline your immune system and makes you mentally weak.

your body do so much for you so it's important to do something for it. Just try doing these things and see the change.

To live a perfect way of life in habits- don't give up! As always. Challenge yourself, like try to do these things for 1 month and lastly make these habits a part of your daily life.

RELATIONSHIPS

Relationships, whether they are good or not play an important role in living a perfect way of life. A child has mostly good relationships because he hasn't started coming into the world yet. As children, many think about their future relationships. Everybody thinks this, so there's no need to feel insecure. It's just natural!

But when children start getting into the real meaning of life; many bad relationships which make us uncomfortable staying with that person start to happen. We don't like that person and don't want to start any relationship with them. we feel insecure, but it's just a part of life. Even though you may have many bad relationships, just forget about them! you need to focus on the good relationships that you have probably with your friend, especially parents, relatives, sisters, brothers, etc.

The thing is some people just overthink, but that's normal too! Do people think that what if my partner leaves me? Or something else like what if my parents never talk to me because of this mistake? Well, the truth is nothing going to happen! You just overthink! We will see in the future what will happen. If you keep thinking like this, days will pass while you still thinking!

Well, in the second example no parent will ever not talk to their child only because of a mistake! Whether it's big or not. Everybody makes mistakes! So just do it! overthinking is just a waste of time. You should just change the way about what you think.

See, there are two types of places in your mind. First where you put the memories which you love. Such as a camping trip with your family, movies and shopping with your friends, etc. put those exquisite things in your mind. then the perfect place for the things that you don't like is…… DUSTBIN! Just like that when you delete unwanted files from your computer. Throw those fights with your partner, bad days, bad memories, etc. in the trash! Don't think about it! and focus on today means NOW!

To live a perfect way of life in relationships- focus on yourself, yourself. Take time to meditate. Forget all those bad relationships and try to make a new, good one. Spend time with your family and friends. Try to control your overthinking by changing the subject to a new nice topic. forget all your bad memories because thinking about your bad memories cannot change the past so just cut it out!!

MENTAL HEALTH

when we talk about mental health then that is very important. mental illness affects you physically. it affects your life. here, I am giving common things that pull us down and how to prevent mental illness.

Overthinking is normal and everyone relates to it. But, much overthinking is not good too. For example in some cases when people start doing a new thing, they start overthinking that what if they fail in it? What if I would not be able to do it? Just cut these negative things out! nothing is going to happen. see, do you know what will happen in the future? no. you don't know. If you won't try then how can you tell what will going to happen?
You can fail your first time because it was your first time. if you practice you can master it!

It's well said that an expert in something was once a beginner. the beginner is now an expert because he/ she tried. kept patience and never gave up! If If you are the rising star of the future then why do you fear? everyone fear. but the most fearest thing is fear itself. you have to face your fears if you want to be successful.

Now let's come to the main topic which is mental health. Mental health refers to cognitive, behavioral, and emotional well-being. It is all about how people think, feel, and behave. here are some tips that how you can take care of your mental health.

- If anything is troubling you, tell it to your trusted adult like your parents, grandparents, etc. it's very important.

- Eat healthily. Eating healthy food can help keep your mental health right.

- Take a break. stress is not good for you. if you feel stressed from your work then a break will help you.

- play puzzles and mind games. a study has shown that playing puzzles can improve cognition and visual-spatial reasoning.

- play some sports. they are fun and good for your brain.

Mental illness

Some early signs of mental illness

- avoiding meeting people or not doing things that they would enjoy.

- feeling hopeless

- eating too much or too little

- sleeping too much or too little

- having low energy

- being confused

- being unable to complete daily tasks

- thinking of causing physical harm to himself or others

treatments for mental illness

- psychotherapy. if you feel you have to see a doctor then meet a psychotherapist

- Medications

- Self-help. eat a balanced diet and sleep well. do meditation and deep breathing exercises.

- if you have pets then spend time with them. Experts have proven then spending time with them releases happy hormones that make us feel better.

I prefer to also take help from your parents or your trusted adults. they will help you feel safe.

to live a perfect way of life in mental health- take care of yourself. Taking help is important. Practicing yoga it's a great way to keep your body and mind healthy.

UNDERSTANDING YOUR TRUE POTENTIAL

Understanding your true potential is extremely important to achieve something. You have to find what is your inner strength. What can you do to make this world better? Now basically first you need to know that there are no shortcuts to the path to success you have to take steps. Step by step you understand yourself and what you can do. First, participate in every competition that you know about. Participating will help you know what is your talent.

You lose it doesn't matter if you participated in those matters. If you think that you cannot do better in that thing, just try a different thing. I participate in every competition that I get to know about. When I participate in one, I already have 2 or more! That is that participating helps to know better of you.

Then to find your true potential you should take the help of everyone that surrounds you they know you better than you think you know. Especially your parents. Ask them what they think of you. That in which field you can do better.

When you know what is your strength and in which field

you do the best; try to participate the most in that field only. Spend time on that field. Suppose, your best fields are music, dance, drawing nay subjects like science, and history. Then, try to spend more time with them. cause the thing is that if you are bad at something like mathematics then you will try to be well at it. but if you will try doing your best in the things which you are best in, it will give you confidence and you can easily master them.

Lastly, don't only focus on your studies, your soft skills should also be perfect. If you are weak in something that is okay! Everyone can't master everything. Don't feel bad that you can't do it. I am very much weak in mathematics but I focus on the things I am nice and your strength are more than your weaknesses.

To live a perfect way of life in understanding your true potential- try giving time to enhance your skills, love yourself, and believe you can do it, if you are weak in something don't worry focus on your good parts. Focus on your soft skills also and in every opportunity and competition, you get to know and participate in it!

LIVING YOUR DREAMS

living your dream is the thing that helps you to live your life the way you want. There's a right time for everything. The earth rotates and completes one day in a specific time of 24 hours. months are also finished at a specific time. Whether things are natural or phenomenal everything has a specific time. Just like that, if you want to live your dream you have to give specific time to it.

you should spend time living your dream. No matter what people say to you. Don't listen to them. Until you know the work you do matches your interest you should keep doing it. Suppose you want to be a dancer or a singer when you grow up then you should practice it in the present. A star isn't born in a day. First, it forms in the nebula from which through gravity it forms a star. This process takes very much time.

Sometimes people don't have support with them. from family and friends but that doesn't mean you will change your dream or your interest. People also win without support. See, it's true that until people see that thing with their own eyes they don't believe in it. but you are the one who will open their eyes. make them realize that the thing they did was wrong.

See, people don't usually support people because of discrimination. it's a really big problem in our society. the change starts with you. you are the future! you will erase discrimination from the book of our society! for that, even though no one supports you; you have to believe in yourself. that yes! I can do it! if you will see, most people who are famous and have achieved very much sometimes feel this way. they go through these problems. but; did they stop? did they leave their dream? NO! because their self-confidence and belief in themselves made them such big people today.

" So no matter who you are, rich or poor, supportless or with support, small or big. you can achieve things! and live the life you want".

" People will say many things to you; DON'T LISTEN! try to be an inspiration for the next generation"

The hard work you'll do today will shape your tomorrow. Sometimes people do hard work but still, they fail and finally quit! You should never quit. In the word 'DON'T QUIT' you'll see that if you remove the 'not' and the' Qu' the word will become do it!
Not one-time hard work and struggles will make you shine. Hard work over many weeks, months, and years will help you. Even if you fail after doing hard work, the more you do it again finally you will reach your goal. When you fail don't just keep crying but try. Crying's not going to change it. but trying will!

" In the work Don't Quit; if you remove 'n't' and 'Qu' it will become DO IT!

Always remember this, don't start crying, keep trying and only then you'll be flying. Now as I have said earlier that you should spend time for yourself and find what is your strength. Just do that and please try to live your dream! Forget about others, focus on you, yourself. Do what you want to do! It's your life! Live the life you love.

To live a perfect way of life in living your dream- do hard work every day to live your dream. A star is not born in one day. Don't quit do it! and lastly value time. It comes one time and then passes like sand so don't waste it!

TAKING CARE OF YOURSELF

Taking care of yourself is extremely important. Your body is magical and it has the power to heal itself but still, it needs proper care because one's the soil loses its fertility it's vanished. So, to take care of yourself follow these steps.

<u>Maintain cleanliness</u>- cleanliness is very much important to stay away from germs. You should bath every day but if you don't feel like bathing or due to some medical issues it's okay to not bath. Don't insist. Then, clean your teeth every day especially at night because all the food that you have eaten all day gets settles at night in your mouth which can cause germs. Avoid eating too much salty or sweet food.

Self-care- you should try some self-care tips to keep your skin, hair, nails, etc. healthy.

- Trim your nails when they get big so you won't get germs in them.

- Apply some face masks for skin protection

- Apply sunscreen when it's too hot because ultraviolet rays can damage your skin

- Keep your hair clean, wash it 3 times a week.

- Wash your face with facewash when it's too dusty.

- Comb your hair every day.

- Eat healthily and reduce the intake of junk.

These were only a few you can try more things for self-care.

<u>Stay green and avoid much screen</u>- you should plant trees and you can also keep nature in your home. Most of you may be having it. then your screen time should be less! It's important. Avoid staying so much on your phone. It has many health hazards everyone knows about it. you should be spending time playing or exercising outdoors it will help you by keeping you fit. Your screen time should be 2 hours a day.

<u>Some disadvantages of screen time</u>

- Physical strain on eyes and body

- Targets sleep

- Increased risk of obesity

- Loss of cognitive ability

- Hand and neck pain

I believe that if something has advantages then disadvantages are there and if something has disadvantages it has advantages too. Now let's see some advantages of staying in nature.

Some advantages of staying in nature

- Reduces anger, fear, and stress

- Give pleasant feelings

- Walks in nature help your memory! One study at the University of Michigan showed participants who took a memory test and then walked in nature did 20 percent better than those who took the test and walk around the city.

- You feel happier according to a Finnish study you feel more psychology restored

- You can concentrate better

- Your vitamin d supply improves when you spend time in the sun

- One study showed that 70-year-old participants who spent time outside every single day had fewer complaints of common aging problems.

- **be happy in what you are-**Everyone is different. So, some could be smart, and some not much. Some are very much sensitive while some are mentally strong. As I have said earlier being different is the thing that makes you special. Even though you may have bad qualities but focus on the good ones. The bad ones will only pull you back. Labeling someone is one of the things that makes you feel negative thoughts. You have to just ignore or if you can't resist anymore, then take an action. A person cannot ignore the thing that makes him uncomfortable for so long. When you feel that now you cannot resist more than just complain about it. If it's in a school or college then you can complaint to your teachers or the principal.

I prefer to wait until three times the person keeps saying it. Because the first time you can ignore, second also. but a third time means he or she is going to do it again and again. Second is when we make a mistake, some sensitive people think about it too much. they think that I will never come to this place again, I will stay at my home only. Well, staying in your comfort zone and not coming out of it can never make you experience it. God has made this world to live in. You go wherever you are and do whatever you want. We think about these things much when we do it many times. Sometimes people can't control their bad habits which make them in trouble. See, it takes years of practice to control your bad habits. Habits don't just go off so easily. You have to keep patience. If you are so much sense that now your mood is so off that you can't be happy again. You can try this:

- take deep breaths

- sit alone in a calm place where there is no noise. You can sit in a room with the door locked or I prefer it in nature.

- you have to defeat those negative thoughts! try to defeat it by thinking good thoughts for example you can say: If it has to happen, it will. I can't change the past, so I have to just forget about it. You can't deny the things which will happen. You can always take help.

- If you have a pet then that is excellent! Experts have found that spending time with your pets can help to battle depression and anxiety. Spending time with them releases happy hormones which help us to feel better.

Well, just try it and see the results.
To live the perfect way of life by taking care of yourself-know more about yourself. You understand yourself the best than any other. Stay patient. If you are sensitive don't feel bad about that. God has made everyone different. Just say, Okay I am ___________ so what? nothing will happen I am happy with what I am.

LETTING GO

Letting go of a thing sometimes feels hard, actually very hard. But nothing is impossible. It feels very hard but it isn't that you can never do it. see, thinking about the most embarrassing moments in the past will not change it. most of all we think that what people will think of us? Well, people just forget it they don't care about it.

If you see someone whose tie has not been tied right what you will do? Just ignore it right? and after a day or so you'll just forget it. it's like that only. People don't pay attention to these things until you do them more often. if you have done something wrong or you feel it was not right; then thinking about it now will not change it. what you can do is to take care that you won't do it again in the future.
See, embarrassing moments in life are common. They are past things. You have to focus on today and that you will take care that you will not do it again.

See, we often feel bad when we can't control our bad habits or mistakes that we did in past. I also have done horrible mistakes many times and sometimes again and again. When I did it at first I just did not take it seriously. but when I did the same mistake a second time too; then I realized that it was bad and to not repeat it.

Sometimes we do a mistake more than two times without realizing it. Do you know how I realized my horrible mistakes? when I told them to my mom and dad. they made me understand that it was okay that I made a mistake but not safe for me so I must not do it again.

You when also will tell your trusted adults about it you will realize it. it's sometimes a very embarrassing or a shameful mistake and you feel afraid to tell but it's normal. we all make shameful and embarrassing moments. the most important thing is that if you feel unsafe after the thing you must tell your parents and trusted adults. the thing could be about anything, like relationships in college, something bad in school, or anything. if you feel unsafe you must tell! it's very much important!

I don't think that your trusted adults, parents especially will scold you. we all make mistakes there's no need to feel shameful. instead, your trusted adults will make you understand, and even though you have done the mistake two times or more in the past; they will never scold you as far as I think. if the mistake has happened in the past many years ago then also don't hide it. Tell! it's never too late to reveal something.

If something bad happens, then don't be sad. Something good will surely happen. Some people have bad things continuously and lose their hope that there's no good going to happen but, if you have bad continuously then one day good will be the same.

Another thing. We all lose our loved ones someday and letting go of that, feels impossible. But the first time you will feel sad very much but as time will pass you will get used to living with the happy memories spent with the ones you have lost. Everyone has to go someday. It's the law of nature but we can't ruin our today because of that. These things have to happen. Of course, you can't bear the feeling but you have to go through it without breaking your dreams.

Just, let it go. Past is past and future is future. You can change the future but not the past and your future depend on the hard work you do today. If you will become lazy or sad now, then the same is going to happen in the future.

To live a perfect way of life in letting go- the past cannot be changed, focus on now and your future. Let go of the embarrassing moments that happened in the past. Always tell. Even though the thing has happened many years ago in the past still tell it! it's never late to tell something.

MOTIVATIONAL QUOTES

PUSH YOURSELF,
BECAUSE NO ONE ELSE
IS GOING TO DO IT
FOR YOU.
SUCCESS.com

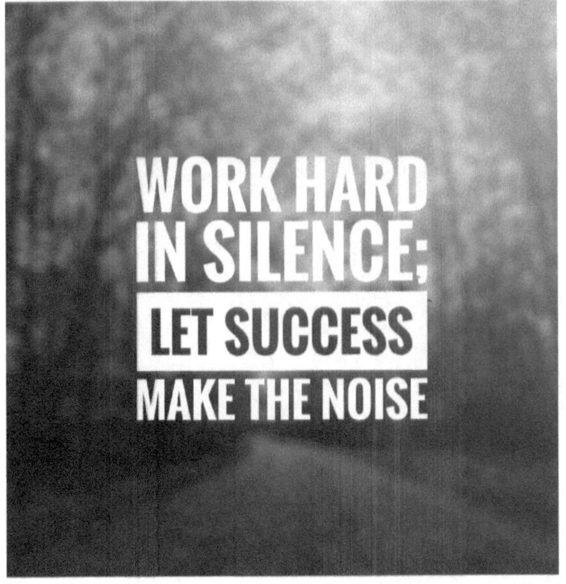
WORK HARD
IN SILENCE;
LET SUCCESS
MAKE THE NOISE

EVERY DAY
IS A CHANGE
TO BE BETTER

THE PAST
Is a place of
LEARNING
Not a place of
LIVING

IT ALWAYS
SEEMS
IMPOSSIBLE
UNTIL IT IS
DONE

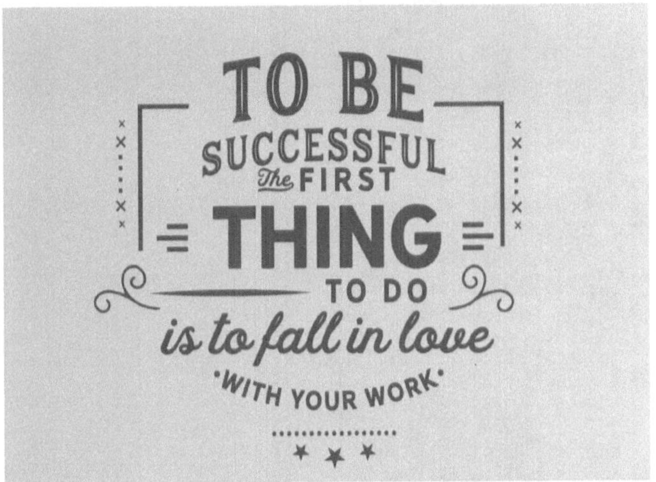
TO BE
SUCCESSFUL
The FIRST
THING
TO DO
is to fall in love
"WITH YOUR WORK"

DON'T
BE AFRAID
TO FAIL.

BE AFRAID
NOT TO TRY.

WHEN LIFE GIVES YOU A
HUNDRED REASONS TO
BREAK DOWN AND CRY,
SHOW LIFE THAT YOU
HAVE A MILLION REASONS
TO SMILE AND LAUGH.
STAY STRONG.

THE MOST
CERTAIN WAY
TO SUCCESS
IS ALWAYS
TO TRY JUST
ONE
MORE
TIME

FUN ACTIVITIES!

<u>Make your to do list!</u>

Date:

1.____
2.____
3.-_______________________________________
4.____
5.____
6.____
7.____
8.____
9.____
10._______________________________________

Date:

1.____
2.____
3.-_______________________________________
4.____
5.____
6.____
7.____
8.____

9.____
10.____

Date:

1.____
2.____
3.-____
4.____
5.____
6.____
7.____
8.____
9.____
10.____

Date:

1.____
2.____
3.-____
4.____
5.____
6.____
7.____
8.____
9.____
10.____

FAVOURITE

HOBBY____

ACTOR____

MOVIE____

SPORTSPERSON_______________________________________

GAME____

SPORTS____

PROFESSION____

CLOTHES____

FOOD____

DRINKS____

THING____

TIME OF THE DAY_____________________________________

SEASON____

NUMBER____

COUNTRY____

NATIONAL TEAM______________________________________

PLACE____

MONUMENT____

SCIENTIST____

PERSON____

ANIMAL____

SUBJECT____

COLOUR____

INFORMATION

NAME____

GENDER____

ADRESS____

MOBILE NO.____

SCHOOL/COLLEGE (IF ANY)___________________

PROFESSION______________________________

BEST

FRIEND_________________________________

HOBBIES________________________________

YOUR SPECIAL WORD________________________

AUTOGRAPH______________________________

SIGNATURE______________________________

YOUR THOUGHT OF THE DAY _________________

YOUR RELATIVES___________________________

FATHER_________________________________

MOTHER________________________________

PET(IF ANY)______________________________

CITY___________________________________

COUNTRY_______________________________

RIDDLES

1.What has to be broken before you can use it?
____

2.What is always in front of you but can't be seen?
____

3.What can you break, even if you never pick it up or touch it? _______________

4.What goes up but never comes down?
____

5.I shave everyday, but my beard stays the same. Who am i? _______________

6.What has many keys but can't open a single lock?

____

7.What is black when it's clean and white when it's dirty?

____

8.What invention lets you look right through a wall?

____

9.What has one eye but can't see?

____

10. What has hands but can't clap?

____

ANSWERS

1.EGG 2. FUTURE 3. A PROMISE 4. YOUR AGE 5. BARBER 6. PIANO 7. CHALKBOARD 8. A WINDOW 9. NEEDLE 10. A CLOCK

www.ingramcontent.com/pod-product-compliance
Lightning Source LLC
LaVergne TN
LVHW091138180726
843490LV00008B/3068